All About You and Your Body

A note for grown-ups

This book is designed to be shared with young children. It celebrates bodies and body diversity and aims to help children maintain a positive body image as they grow up.

At the back of the book, you'll find more ideas for how to help children develop body confidence and keep feeling good about themselves whatever their shape, size, age and ability. There's also information about how to access **Usborne Quicklinks** for further advice.

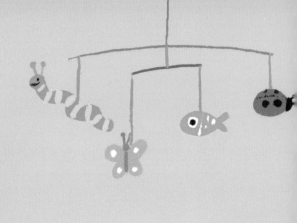

Contents

Usborne

All About You and Your Body

Felicity Brooks

Illustrated by Mar Ferrero

Designed by Frankie Allen

With expert advice from Dr. Kristina Routh, MBChB, MPH

Our amazing bodies

Human bodies are ALL amazing. Have you ever thought about all the different things YOUR body can do? Maybe you can . . .

think

I wonder what's for lunch?

sit

stand

kneel

jump

LAAAAAAA!

sing

clap

dance

SNO-O-O-O-RE!

sleep

hug

Where's my teddy bear?

cry

worry

pee and poop

You can probably do many of these things, but could you do all of them when you were a little baby? Which ones do you think you had to learn? Turn the page to find out . . .

Growing and changing

Maybe you turned this page by using your fingers to grip the paper. This is something you have learned to do, as well as many, many other things since you were a little baby.

WAAAAAAAA!

1 Tiny babies can only suck milk, sleep, pee, poop and cry ... A LOT!

2 At around 6 months, many learn to roll.

6 It takes a LOT of tries before they can stand up by themselves ...

LA LA LAAA! Sing, bunny!

Bus!

7 ...and LOTS of practice to learn to walk and say words.

8 LOTS MORE to learn to how to talk and sing ...

You may not remember learning any of this, but you learned more in the first two years of your life than you will at any other time. And all the time you are learning, you are using your brain and . . .

Your senses

Your **senses** help you find out about the world and understand what's around you. All the information that they send to your brain helps you to learn. These are the five main senses.

You SMELL things with your nose – both good and bad!

SIGHT is being able to see. You see things with your eyes.

You HEAR sounds with your ears.

You TOUCH with your skin.

You TASTE things with your tongue.

Not everyone can use all five senses. This may be because they have a **sensory impairment** or a **disability** and might need special equipment or some extra help.

If someone can't see or can't see very well, they are **blind** or **sight impaired**. Glasses help some people to see better.

If someone can't hear well or at all, they have hearing loss or are **deaf**. They may use **sign language** to talk to their friends.

People sometimes lose their sense of taste and smell when they're sick. This is usually only for a short time.

Sensory overload is when your senses take in more information at the same time than your brain can cope with.

You're using your senses all the time, often without even thinking about it. Which sense are you using if you are looking at the pictures in this book?

How bodies communicate

Our bodies are great at swapping information, or communicating, and have all kinds of ways of doing it. We need to communicate to talk to friends, let people know how we're feeling, and find out about things.

Your **facial expression** (the look on your face) can show how you feel. How do you think these children are feeling?

A **gesture** is an action you do with your hands or another part of your body to communicate something.

Your whole body shape or **posture** also communicates things to other people – sometimes without you knowing about it! This is known as **body language.**

Wide open arms and a smiling face make this boy look friendly and happy.

What do this girl's face and curled up body shape communicate to you?

What about this man's body language, with his hands on his hips?

You make sounds and words with your mouth, and your voice box or **larynx**. They let you control sounds so that you can talk, SHOUT, whisper, and make many other kinds of noises. But we can't control some noises that come out of our bodies!

Your larynx is in your neck.

Shhh! We need to be very quiet!

WEE-OH WEE-OH

NOT FAIR!

BURP!

Wheeeee!

Want to ride with me?

BRRRING!

Yes, please!

EXIT →

Your ears let you listen to what other people are saying, and your brain lets you make sense of sounds and words.

Visual communication is using pictures, signs, and symbols. Your eyes and brain help you understand what they mean.

Next time you're out and about, see if you can spot people using some of these different ways of communicating.

All bodies are different

A fantastic thing about human bodies is that they come in all sorts of shapes, sizes, and ages, and with many different kinds and colors of skin, eyes, and hair.

Skin can be black, brown, or white and many shades in between. Everyone gets their skin color from their **birth parents** and **ancestors**.

Anyone else for ice cream?

Thanks!

I have a new shirt!

Some people have scars, birthmarks, freckles, patches, rashes, or spots on their skin.

People like to wear all kinds of different clothes.

At this busy market, can you spot someone who . . .

- is wearing green shorts
- has very long hair
- is using a **mobility aid** to get around
- has a beard
- has pictures called tattoos on their skin
- has a **prosthetic** leg
- is **pregnant** (going to have a baby)
- is a grown-up little person
- is bald (has no hair)

Hair can be curly, coily, straight, wavy, frizzy, spiky, fine, thick, long, or short ... what's yours like?

Some people have a limb difference. (Limbs are your arms and legs.) They may use a **prosthetic** arm or leg.

Someone who has a **disability** may need a **mobility aid** such as a walker to get around.

Hello, Nana!

Hello, sweetheart!

Bodies change as they get older. What differences can you see between all the people in this family?

Whatever your body is like, it's special because it's yours and because it keeps you alive! Can you draw a picture of YOUR fantastic body?

What your body needs

To be able to grow, do so many amazing things, and feel happy and well, your brain and body need A LOT of help. These are some of the different things they need every day.

MY BODY NEEDS...

Try out some different foods and eat lots of fruit and vegetables.

Don't forget to drink lots of water!

SOMETHING TO DRINK
Your body and brain need plenty of water to stay well. You may even get a headache if you don't drink enough.

GOOD FOOD
Food helps your body and brain work correctly and keeps your bones strong. It gives you energy and **nutrients** that help you grow and stay well.* When you are hungry, you can feel grumpy.

FRESH AIR
Nobody can live without breathing in something called oxygen that's in the air. Everything we do, such as moving or even just thinking, needs oxygen.

POOP PROBLEMS?
Not drinking enough water can make you feel a little grumpy. It can even stop you from pooping easily!

*You can find out more about what kinds of food your body needs on page 18.

EXERCISE AND PLAY

Exercise is anything that gets you moving and it's really good for your body! You need about three hours of exercise and play every day.

You could skip, run, swim, jump, dance, cycle, ride a scooter...

MY TOP BOOKS

Dinosaur book

Fingerpaint book

Bugs sticker book

WOW! I never knew that!

THINKING AND LEARNING

Your brain needs to keep learning new things to work at its best. If you're not thinking and learning, you may feel a little bored and unhappy.

A SAFE PLACE

You need somewhere to sleep, wash, eat, play, stay warm and dry, and be with your family or carers. Feeling safe and loved helps you to be happy and well and stops you from worrying too much.

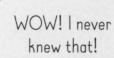

HOME SWEET HOME

LOTS OF SLEEP

When you don't get enough sleep, you may feel a little grumpy and sad, as well as tired. This makes it harder to learn things and to remember new words. Sleep even helps your body to GROW!

DID YOU KNOW?
When you are young, you need about 12 hours of sleep every night.

Night-night, sleep tight!

Your feelings and your body

Your body has all kinds of ways of showing feelings that are inside your head. Sometimes it even does things that you can't control.

She's feeling HAPPY.

They are feeling SAD.

She feels NERVOUS.

Some things that happen to your body tell you that it needs something.

Yawning shows that your body is TIRED and needs some sleep.

Shivering tells you that your body is COLD and needs to warm up.

Sweating a lot shows that you are HOT and need to find a way to cool down.

These children are telling you about the things they do to feel happier or calmer when they have a feeling they don't like.

WOW!

I look at my favorite book.

Your fur is so soft.

PURRRRRR

I pet my cat.

It's OK. It's OK.

I tell myself that it's all OK and I am doing my best.

Mmmm... you smell so nice.

I hug my teddy bear.

I think of a place that I really like.

And then I felt like...

1...2...3...

I take deep breaths in and out, counting slowly.

I talk to my grandma and tell her all about my worries.

Is there something you like to do to feel calm?

Taking care of your amazing body

Your body only works well if you take really good care of it. These children are giving you some tips about some things you need to do to look after your body and keep it safe and well.

NEVER play with sharp things like knives and scissors.

Stay away from hot things that could burn you.

Don't eat or drink ANYTHING unless you know that it's safe.

If you feel sick or hurt yourself, tell your grown-up.

SOB!

Don't go near a dog unless the owner says it's OK.

If you pull a cat's tail, it might scratch you!

HISS!

Hold your grown-up's hand when you cross the road.

We cross at the crosswalk.

Don't run or play near the road.

ZOOOOOM!

Only climb on things that are meant for climbing.

Don't push or shove other people when you're playing.

Ha ha!

Hee hee!

Don't forget to hold on tight!

Clothes and getting dressed

To keep your body comfortable and safe, try to choose clothes that are right for the weather and for what you are going to be doing.

On a cold day, you need thick clothes to keep warm when you go outside.

Thin clothes and sandals are good for hot weather and help you stay cool.

On a wet day, you need boots, and a hood to keep your head dry.

I love the snow!

Warm hat

Scarf

Mittens

Warm coat

Don't forget your hat!

Sandals

Hood

Raincoat

Boots

SPLAAAAASH!

Sports clothes are good for running around and getting sweaty.

Shinpads under socks protect your legs for soccer.

Sneakers are good for running.

Shorts

Night clothes keep you comfortable in bed.

These pajamas feel soft!

Swimwear can get wet, and dries quickly.

Floatation vest

Swim cap

My swimsuit stops my skin from burning in the sun.

Goggles protect your eyes.

Some clothes help keep the rest of your clothes clean so you can have fun getting messy.

Helmets keep your head safe if you fall.

Jaden is getting dressed to go outside on a cold, dry day. Which clothes do you think he should choose? What should he put on first?

If you like, you could find a piece of paper and draw a picture of some clothes you'd really like to wear.

Getting sick

Even if you take really good care of your body, sometimes things go wrong and you get sick. You know you are sick when you have some signs or **symptoms**, such as . . .

a tummy ache

a headache or earache

spots or an itchy rash

ITCH ITCH

a sore throat, cough, or runny nose

If you notice any of these things happening to your body, tell your grown-up straightaway.

a temperature

I feel too hot!

having no energy

feeling sick or throwing up

BLEURRGH

SPLAT!

runny poop

Many sicknesses are caused by **germs**. Germs live in lots of places – in food, on the things around us, and even inside us. Most of the time our bodies can fight off the harmful ones, but sometimes the germs win for a while.

Germs are much too tiny to see, but they love to spread. They can easily move from a sick person to another person and make the other person sick, too.

When germs make you sneeze, some float off into the air . . .

. . . if another person breathes them in, the germs spread.

Germs can also come from things we touch, and from poop.

STOP THOSE GERMS!

Use a tissue when you cough or sneeze . . .

. . . then throw the tissue away.

Wash your hands after you have used the toilet, and before you touch food.

Some people get symptoms because they have an **allergy**, or another health condition.

My inhaler helps me breathe more easily.

Hay fever gives you itchy eyes and makes you sneeze.

ACHOO!

Asthma is a health condition that can sometimes make it hard to breathe.

Hay fever is an allergy to a powder called pollen that comes from grass and flowers.

Do you have any allergies or a health condition?
If you do, what do you need to do to make sure you stay well?

Getting better

When you're sick, you often just need to rest and let your grown-ups take care of you. But sometimes you need to see a doctor to find out what's wrong. These children are pretending to be doctors to show what happens.

First, a doctor asks what the problem is.

Hello! I'm Doctor Rani. How can I help you, Miss Bear?

This won't hurt at all.

Then she might ask more questions and check your body. She may . . .

. . . use a **stethoscope** to listen to your breathing,

. . . use a **thermometer** to check your temperature,

Say "ahhh", monkey!

He needs one spoonful three times a day.

. . . look into your mouth to see if your throat is sore,

. . . check your ears with an **otoscope**,

. . . say you need some **medicine** and tell your grown-up how much to give you.

NEVER, EVER take any medicines by yourself – always ask your grown-up first.

Your medicine could be . . .

a liquid or a pill that you swallow,

a cream that you rub on your skin,

or some drops for your eyes.

Sometimes you see a doctor or nurse to have a **vaccination.** Vaccinations teach your body how to fight off dangerous germs that could make you ill.

If you get a little cut or graze, you don't need a doctor. Your grown-up can clean the **wound.** They may put on a bandage or dressing to keep it clean.

If you have a more serious illness or a big **injury,** such as a broken bone, you need to go to a hospital. The hospital doctors and nurses will help you get better.

You don't always have to stay at the hospital overnight. But if you do, your grown-ups can stay with you all the time until you are better.

Can you think of a time you were sick? Did you go to a doctor or hospital? What did you need to do to get better?

What's it called?

These are the names for some of the different parts of the body. Do you know the words for all of them?

Can you point to these parts on your body?

Head

Hand

I was born without a hand on one arm.

Tummy

Bottom

Foot

Elbow

Leg

Knee

Fingers

Shoulder

Toes

I have paws and a tail!

I call my vulva "noonie."

I call my penis "doodle."

Your genitals are the parts between your legs. Most girls have a vulva, and vagina (which is inside their body). Most boys have a penis and testicles.

People sometimes call genitals your "private parts" (but you can call yours whatever you want).

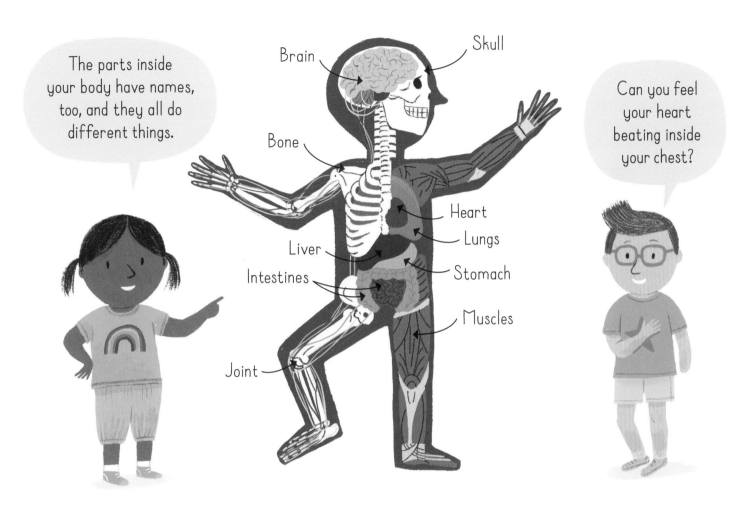

The parts inside your body have names, too, and they all do different things.

Can you feel your heart beating inside your chest?

Brain

Skull

Bone

Heart

Lungs

Liver

Stomach

Intestines

Muscles

Joint

Alex and Yaz have drawn pictures of themselves to show the parts of their heads and faces.

Hair

Eye

Ear

Cheek

Mouth

Tongue

Forehead

Nose

Chin

Lips

Neck

Teeth

Can you draw a picture of your face? What color are your eyes? What is your hair like? What shape is your mouth?

Your body is your own

Your body belongs to you, and you can choose what happens to it. You don't have to be hugged, kissed, tickled, or touched by anyone (even someone in your family) if you are not comfortable with it.

Some people like to hug, but they should always ask you if it's OK so you can choose.

If you decide you do want to hug, you need to say "YES." This is called giving **consent**.

If you don't want to hug, it's OK. You could high five, wave, say "hello," or fist bump instead.

Here are some things to remember to keep your body safe and help you to stay happy.

PRIVATE PARTS ARE PRIVATE...

Your underwear or swimsuit covers your private parts. No one should ask to see or touch them.

You shouldn't touch another person's private parts (even if they ask you to) as they are private, too.

A doctor, nurse, or your special grown-ups (the people who take care of you) may sometimes need to see your private parts, but they should ask if it's OK first.

TELL SOMEONE...

If someone tries to see or touch your private parts or does anything that hurts you or makes you feel uncomfortable, TELL YOUR GROWN-UP.

It's ALWAYS good to talk about things that upset, scare, or worry you.

TALK ABOUT "BAD" SECRETS...

Good secrets (like a surprise present) make us feel happy and excited, but bad ones make us feel uncomfortable or unsafe.

No one should ask you to keep a bad secret — especially if it's about private parts. If a secret makes you feel worried, TELL YOUR GROWN-UP.

AND NEVER FORGET THAT...

Your body is your own, and you are allowed to say "NO" even to someone you love.

ALL bodies are different, and all bodies are good!

You don't need to be like anyone except you. YOU ARE AMAZING just as you are!

It's important to FEEL GOOD about your body whatever you can do and whatever your size, shape, age, and color.

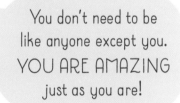

You'll live in your body your WHOLE LIFE, so you need to take care of it and keep it safe.

Some useful body words

Allergy – If you have an allergy to something, it could make you sick if you eat, breathe, or touch it.

Ancestors – relatives who lived a long time ago

Birth parents – the parents someone had when they were born

Blind – Someone who is blind has a **disability** that means they are unable to see.

Body language – a kind of communication that uses body signals and movements such as **facial expressions**, body **posture**, and hand **gestures**

Consent – when you give permission or agree that something can happen by saying "yes" to it

Deaf – Someone who is deaf has a **disability** that means they are unable to hear.

Disability – any condition of someone's body or brain that may make it more difficult for them to do some activities, communicate, or learn. There are many different kinds of disabilities and different reasons for them. A disability can affect someone's **senses**, movement, thinking, understanding, memory, learning, communication, and so on. You can't always see that someone has a disability.

Facial expression – a type of communication where the look on someone's face shows that they are happy, angry, sad, surprised, and so on

Germs – tiny things such as some bacteria and viruses that can make people sick

Gesture – a movement of a part of the body to communicate an idea or message

Injury – damage to a part of someone's body, often caused by an accident

Larynx – the "voice box" inside someone's neck that allows them to make sounds and speak

Medicines – things such as pills, liquids, injections, and creams that may help people get better when they are sick, manage a health condition, or stop them from getting sick.

Mobility aid – a piece of equipment, such as a wheelchair, walking frame, crutch, or walking stick that helps someone to get around more easily, especially if they have a **disability** or an **injury**

Nutrient – something in food that everyone needs to stay strong and healthy. Vitamins are nutrients.

Otoscope – an instrument that doctors use to look inside people's ears. It has a magnifying lens and a light to help the doctor see if anything's wrong.

Posture – the way you hold your body when you are standing, sitting, or lying down

Pregnant – Someone who is pregnant is going to give birth to a baby. Pregnancy lasts about nine months.

Prosthetic (or **prosthesis**) – a specially made body part that someone may sometimes wear because their body is shaped differently at birth, or after an accident or health problem

Senses – Your senses allow you to find out about and understand the world. The five main senses are sight, hearing, smell, touch, and taste.

Sensory impairment – when one or more of someone's **senses** doesn't work as well as others

Sensory overload – when someone's **senses** take in more information at the same time than their brain can cope with

Sight impaired – unable to see as well as before or as well as some other people,

Sign language – a language for communicating using hand and body movements, and **facial expressions**, rather than spoken words. There are more than 300 different sign languages used around the world, especially by people who are **deaf**.

Stethoscope – an instrument that doctors use for listening to someone's heartbeat or breathing

Symptom – something such as a sore throat or high temperature that shows someone is unwell

Thermometer – an instrument that can be used for measuring temperature

Vaccination – a **medicine** (usually an injection) that protects people against dangerous **germs**

Visual communication – communication that uses pictures, signs, and symbols, and not words

Wound – a cut, graze, scratch, or other **injury** that breaks someone's skin or another body part

Some notes for grown-ups

This book celebrates bodies and body diversity (differences) and aims to help young children develop confidence in their bodies and maintain a positive body image as they grow. Body image is how someone thinks and feels about their body, how it works, and what it looks like – their size, shape, skin color, and weight for example. Body image has a huge impact on emotional, social, and physical wellbeing, and starts to develop as soon as toddlers begin to recognize themselves in the mirror or in a photo.

It's now known that body confidence in the early years lays the foundations for a positive body image and good health and wellbeing in the teenage years, so it's vital that we help children develop body confidence from a young age. When children feel good about their bodies, they're more likely to enjoy healthy food, stay healthy, keep themselves clean, and feel good about themselves in general as they grow up. By contrast, a negative body image may contribute to a range of problems in later life, including low self-esteem, depression, and disordered eating.

Help your child maintain a healthy body image

Some good starting points to help children develop body confidence are to encourage them to appreciate their bodies and what they can do; celebrate similarities and differences; help them identify what they like about themselves; and teach them how to look after their bodies and keep them safe.

Studies have shown that negative comments about a child's appearance from family members and friends can cause lifelong insecurities, and the way adults talk about bodies and food around children can have a lasting effect. Children as young as three pay close attention to how those around them behave and talk about bodies, so it's important to role model body positivity around young children to inspire them to feel confident and happy about their own bodies:

* Avoid commenting on what children look like and focus on what they can do, what they enjoy, and what they are interested in.

* Make a point of praising children when they are kind, help others, or try hard, for example. This shows that you value who they are and recognize their skills rather than focusing on appearance.

* Pause before commenting on any child's appearance or clothes ("What a pretty dress!") and think of something else you like about them. ("Great to see you. We always have a lot of fun when you're around!")

* Avoid expressing dissatisfaction with your own body, talking about weight, going on diets, or wanting to change your body when you're around children.

* Remember that the more you focus on weight being a problem or certain foods being "bad," the more guilt, shame, and body dissatisfaction young children are likely to develop.

* Avoid comparing your body and appearance to others, and talk about exercise being important for health and wellbeing rather than as a way to lose weight.

* Make eating healthy family meals a normal everyday activity rather than talking about specific foods being good or bad for you.

* Be positive and appreciative of your own body and what it can do. ("I really love my feet. They've walked such a long way today!") Encourage children to do the same.

* Jump in if you hear children talking about other people's bodies in unkind or negative ways, or teasing anyone based on their looks. (You could ask them how it would make them feel if someone made similar comments about theirs.)

* Talk about how bodies all look different and that's a fantastic thing.

* Look for books which feature diverse characters and celebrate diverse bodies and abilities.

* Monitor what children watch or see on screens, making sure it is age-appropriate, and try to watch tv shows and movies that include diverse characters and positive role models.

* Encourage your child to talk about their feelings. If they feel it's safe to talk, they are more likely to share feelings about their bodies.

Body parts and body boundaries

If you are comfortable, use and teach the correct terms for body parts, including genitals, and try to be open about answering any questions. You don't have to go into great detail, but don't brush away children's questions.

Be clear about who is allowed to see or touch their genitals (for example, "Only dad and me and a nurse or doctor are allowed to see your penis when we are taking care of you.") Make sure they know exactly who their "special" (trusted) grown-ups are so they know who they can talk to if anything is worrying them.

Read through the "rules" about consent and "private parts" on pages 28 and 29 with your children and check that they understand them. It's completely normal for young children to touch their own genitals, so don't worry if they do, but help them understand that this isn't something they should do in public.

Usborne Quicklinks

Scan the QR code, or go to **usborne.com/Quicklinks** and type in the keywords **all about your body** for links to websites with activities and videos to share with young children about bodies and body image. There's also helpful advice for grown-ups about how to deal with a child's negative body image, bullying, or worries about body boundaries.

Children should be supervised online. Please read our internet safety guidelines at Usborne Quicklinks.

Usborne Publishing is not responsible for the availability or content of any website other than its own, or for any exposure to harmful, offensive or inaccurate material which may appear on the Web.